ORGANISING STRATEGY OF THE PROPHET (ﷺ)

Prof Javed Iqbal Saani, PhD
PhD, MBA (MIS), MBA (Finance), BBA

Intellectual Capital Enterprise Limited, London

Copyright © 2018 Prof Javed Iqbal Saani, PhD

All rights reserved.

No reproduction of the book in any form such as electronic, photocopying, scanning, recording or otherwise. It also includes storing for retrieval purposes or transmitting through electronic media i.e., email. Prior written permission of the publisher may require doing any of the above under the relevant act that follows the Copyright, Design, and Patent Act 1988.

Authors and the publisher are not responsible for any damage caused by the application/use of the concepts, techniques, instruction, or actions. The authors and the publisher refuse any implied warranties or related matters.

ISBN: 9781726320245

Published by Intellectual Capital Enterprise Limited
ICE Kemp House, 152-160 City Road
London, EC1 V2N
Printed in England

CONTENTS

About the author	VII
Dedication	XIII
Acknowledgement	XV
PREFACE	XVII

1 THE BASICS OF ORGANIZING. — 1

Introduction	1
Division of work	2
Definition of sub-tasks	3
Managerial triangle	5
Line and staff authority	9
Chain of support/command	10
Harmony among members	13
Treatment of subordinates	14

2 ORGANISATION STRUCTURE — 19

Introduction	19
Departmentalisation	20
Department of defence	21

Departments of Education and Finance	22
Span of control	23
Organisation structure	25

3 RESOURCE ALLOCATION — 31

Introduction	31
Allocation of resources	31
Individuals and Teams	35
Team formation	36

4 COMMUNICATION — 41

Introduction	41
Channels of communication	42
Written communication	44
Nonverbal	45
Innovative elements	47
Attentive listener	49
Correction of mistakes	50

5 CASE STUDY – THE BATTLE OF UHAD — 53

Introduction	53

The initial preparations	54
Organisation of the workforce	55
Encouragement	59
Strategic action	60

6 MANAGERIAL IMPLICATIONS 63

Introduction	63
Definition of roles and responsibilities	65
The physical layout of the facilities	68
Departmentalisation	69
Human resource management	71
Selection of personnel	73
Communication strategy	74
BIBLIOGRAPHY	77
INDEX	81
OTHER BOOKS BY THE AUTHOR (S)	87

About the author

Dr. Javed Iqbal belongs to Rawalakot district Poonch Azad Kashmir. He received his early education from Pilot High School Rawalakot and received his matriculation in 1975 and intermediate from Hussain Shaheed Degree College of the same town. He earned BBA with a gold medal and an MBA with a gold medal from Azad Jammu and Kashmir University in 1986. He was appointed as a lecturer in Business Administration in the same university. Later, he was selected by the government of Pakistan for higher studies and deputed to the United Kingdom. He received MBA from the University of Hull and PhD from the University of Salford. Dr Iqbal has been working in England in various capacities: professor, director of studies, marketing advisor and academic advisor. Dr Iqbal returned to Home in 2006 and joined Iqra University Islamabad campus as an associate professor. He became the head of department of technology Management in International Islamic University Islamabad (IIUI). He went back to England for some time and re-joined IIUI in 2012. He is a Professor of Business Administration in Iqra University, Islamabad, and an

Adjunct Professor in the School of Management in Asia e University Malaysia these days.

He is a distinguished teacher and world known scholar. His article title "Learning from a Doctoral Research Project: Structure and Content of a Research Proposal" has been ranked by one of the professors at Deakin University Australia as the best piece of knowledge for doctoral students on the subject. This paper is widely used and referred all over the world. Dr. Javed Iqbal has been nominated by an international organization for the Award of Distinguished Scientist for his research contribution. His books on various subjects are available on amazon.

Value of knowledge

Say (to them, O Muhammad): Are those who know equal with those who know not? But only men of understanding will pay heed. [Az-Zumar: 9]

Anas (May Allah be pleased with him) reported: The Messenger of Allah (ﷺ) said, "He who goes forth in search of knowledge is considered as struggling in the Cause of Allah until he returns." [At- Tirmidhi].

Abu'd-Darda' (رضي الله عن) said, "I heard the Messenger of Allah, may Allah bless him and grant him peace, say,
1. 'Allah will make the path to the Garden easy for anyone who travels a path in search of knowledge.
2. Angels spread their wings for the seeker of knowledge out of pleasure for what he is doing.
3. Everyone in the heavens and everyone in the earth asks forgiveness for a man of knowledge, even the fish in the water.
4. The superiority of the man of knowledge to the man of worship is like the superiority of the moon to all the planets.
5. The men of knowledge are the heirs of the Prophets.
6. The Prophets bequeath neither dinar nor dirham; they bequeath knowledge. Whoever takes it has taken an ample portion.'"

[Abu Dawud and at-Tirmidhi; Riyadh us Salihin, Hadith 1388, p. 211]

How to manage people?

It was by the mercy of God that you were lenient with them (O Muhammad), for if you had been severe and hard-hearted, they would have forsaken you. So, pardon them and ask (God's) forgiveness for them and consult with them upon the conduct of affairs. [Al-e-Imran: 159]

Dedication

To the entire Ummah who have embraced the message of the prophet (ﷺ) and is sacrificing because they proclaim that Allah (سبحانه و تعالى) is their Rubb, Quran is their book and Muhammad (ﷺ) is their prophet (ﷺ), the leader.

XIV

Acknowledgement

I am obliged to my family who spared me to embark on the project. They also provide valuable information which enriched the contents of this effort. May Allah reward them for their contribution? Ameen!

PREFACE

Allah (سبحانه و تعالى), the exalted, the most gracious, the most merciful, the most knowledgeable, bestowed upon His message upon His most beloved creation, the leader of prophets (AS), benefactor of the humans and a blessing for both worlds. He is the source of guidance to seek the pleasure of our creator, the sustainer, and the controller of our affairs. He has shown the perfect path that leads towards paradise, the ultimate aboard of those who embrace the message of the truthful, sacrificed their lives and belongings for the purpose. The mercy of Allah (سبحانه و تعالى) to the team of the prophet (AS) who followed the noble footsteps of our and their beloved leader and offered everything that they had for the cause of Islam. It encompasses every sphere of human activity whether individual or collective at a small level or at a large level.

Mankind had been managing its affairs since the inception of life on the planet. Prophets (AS) were chosen people who received guidance from Allah (سبحانه و تعالى) who is ever watching, knowing, and managing the universe. The knowledge of the prophets (AS) is extremely high which is not attainable by a common person. Each action they take, they did it with the guidance of Allah (سبحانه و تعالى). So, there is no chance of mistake for them.

Since management science is one of the recent disciplines, therefore, little research has been conducted in Islamic perspective. This book is an attempt towards it. Contemporary managers manage their organisations on the bases of available knowledge and practices. Experts had divided their job into four well-known parts. Planning, organising, leading, and controlling. I have authored a research paper about planning in Islamic perspective in 2009 with one of my colleagues. It was a brief account of the subject. Therefore, I thought it needs expansion. Consequently, a book on the "Planning Strategy of the Prophet [PBUH]" was published recently. One of the reviewers of one of my books on a similar subject suggested that small books must be produced based upon the life of the prophet (ﷺ). And it is the second effort towards it.

First four chapters are dealing with the subject with reference to various aspects of the life of the prophet (ﷺ) with organising perspective. The examples were drawn from various dimensions of the noble autobiography of the prophet (ﷺ). The fifth chapter is reserved to a specific instance; the case study. The last chapter deals with the managerial implications extracted from the case study. Managers can apply them in the future planning endeavours.

Finally, if something is good for the reader it is the mercy and favour of Allah (سبحانه و تعالى); however, all mistakes go to my account. I ask forgiveness from Allah (سبحانه و تعالى) for this. He is merciful, I hope He would forgive me whether they are intentional or unintentional mistakes.

Professor Javed Iqbal Saani, Ph. D
Manchester
August 20, 2018

1 The Basics of organizing.

Introduction

The second managerial function is to organize the workforce and resources in a manner useful for the organization. Managers are supposed to optimize outcome within the managerial and financial constraints such as bounded rationality or sacred cow.

Organising encompasses chain of command, a division of labour and assignment of responsibilities to individuals and teams (Kreiter, 2009).

Box 1 Case of a Muslim manager

Performance of individual tasks is one of the fundamental responsibilities of a Muslim. The job of a leader is to facilitate it. Take the example of salat; it is compulsory for a Muslim as an individual, but imam or ruler ensures its performance. Since leaders in Islam also lead a congregation of salah, therefore, he makes it happen on time in the masjid.

It suggests that the Muslim manager needs to fix the time of salat, the moazzin, the imam and the venue.

Experts believe that a manager needs to address some key issues such as:

1. How will the manager divide the organisation?
2. Who will report to whom?
3. How will the manager distribute the workload?
4. What will be the responsibilities of individual and teams?
5. What will be the accountability mechanism?[1]

Let us examine them in the following pages.

Division of work

A successful organisation completes its work activities in the best way. It implies breaking down the overall work of the organisation in the

---

[1] Dyck and Neubert, p. 295-96.

individual sub-tasks. And identify the best way to perform each sub-task. The prophet (ﷺ) had conceptualised the overall work at the occasion of the installation of Black Stone. He divided the work among major stakeholders i.e. the leaders of various clans. At the time of digging the trench, he assigned 10 individuals a specific piece of land for digging.

A related issue with the phenomenon is to standardise the work practice for every member of the work group. We understand that the prophet (ﷺ) was a messenger of Allah (سبحانه و تعالى), the exalted. In this connection, he had to establish the system of worship along with other matters. The system of worship guides about work practices. For instance, salah offers uniformity of actions and timings. It teaches equality and brotherhood. Thus, the prophet (ﷺ) introduced the uniform practice of getting together and engage in an act of common interest. Hajj and fasting in Ramadan also augment the same idea.

Definition of sub-tasks

Ensure that sub-tasks contribute to the whole and each member understands his work.[1] The

---

[1] Dyck and Neubert, p. 295.

prophet (ﷺ) set up a team of 50 archers as a sub-team at Uhad to guard a certain entry point of the enemy. Molana Muhammad Zakerya writes in this connection:

> Despite heavy odds, the Muslims were gaining the upper hand when some people made a blunder and the Muslims had to suffer a reverse. The Prophet (ﷺ) (Sallallaho alaihe wasallam) had posted a band of fifty archers to guard a pass in the rear against the enemy cavalry. They had definite instructions not to move from their position till further orders from him. But when they saw the Muslims gaining victory and the enemy in full flight, they left their position in the belief that the battle was over, and it was time to join in the pursuit and get on to the booty. The leader of the band tried his utmost to check them by reminding them of the Prophet's (ﷺ) (Sallallaho alaihe wasallam) command and solicited them to stay on, but no more than ten persons would listen to him, arguing that the orders given by the Prophet (ﷺ) (Sallallaho alaihe wasallam) were only for the duration of the actual fight. The enemy cavalry then noticed the unguarded pass in the rear, made a flank movement, forced a passage

through it, and fell right on the rear of the Muslims, who were pre-occupied with the booty.[1]

The mainstream army units were engaged with the opponents but this team was looking after a specific post.

Mainstream managers create sub-tasks (Dyck and Neubert, 2009). It implies creating separate jobs for each member. The prophet (ﷺ) had allocated many jobs for his companions. He appointed Abi bin Ka'b (رضي الله عنه) for writing the revelations. And he has deputed various people for collecting zakat.[2]

Managerial triangle

Three concepts in management work in a sequence: authority, responsibility, and accountability. Authority is the formal "right to direct the actions of others" (Kreitner: 2009). The prophet (ﷺ) himself enjoyed the authority when he placed the Black Stone at its designated position. He assigned authority to Usman (رضي الله عنه) to talk to Quraysh about a peace pact at the occasion of Hodabia. It implies that Usman (رضي الله عنه) was than responsible

---

[1] Fazail-e-Amaal,
[2] Naomani and Nadvi, 1995.

for the job because responsibility "is the obligation or duty of members to perform assigned task" (Dyck and Neubert: 2009). Consequently, accountability emerged. The prophet (ﷺ) deputed Hozaifa (رضي الله عنه) When Hozaifa (رضي الله عنه) returned for informational assessment at the time of the war of Trench, Hozaifa (رضي الله عنه) returned and presented his report of the visit to the prophet (ﷺ).

> Huzaifah (رضي الله عنه) narrates: "In the war of the Trench … One night, during those difficult days, it was unusually very dark and windy. It was so dark that one could not see one's own hand, and the wind was blowing wildly. The Munafiqin were returning to their homes. Three hundred of us were sticking to our positions. Nabi (Sallallahu Alayhi Wasallam) approached everyone and made enquiries about him. I had neither arm to defend myself, nor clothes to resist the cold. I had only one small sheet, which belonged to my wife and was lent to me. I wrapped it round my loins and sat with my knees clinging to the ground. When Nabi (Sallallahu Alayhi Wasallam) passed by me, he said, 'Who are you?' I said, 'Huzaifah!' I could not stand up due to the severe cold and I clung to the ground

more tightly with shame. He said, 'Huzaifah, stand up and go to the enemy camp and bring us their news.' Of all the Sahaabah (رضي الله عنه), I was the most ill-equipped, both against the enemy and against the cold that night, but as soon as I got the order, I stood up and left for the enemy camp. As I was going, Nabi (Sallallahu Alayhi Wasallam) made Dua for me saying, 'Oh Allah! Protect him from all directions.' Immediately after his Dua, I was completely relieved of my fear and cold. I felt as if I were walking in a warm and peaceful atmosphere. Nabi (Sallallahu Alayhi Wasallam) warned me thus, 'Return immediately after seeing what they are doing. Do not take any other step.' When I reached the enemy camp, I found a fire burning and people sitting around it. Each person warmed his hands before the fire and then rubbed them over his body. The shouts of "Go Back" were heard from all directions. Everyone was shouting to the people of his family to pack up and go back. The wind was causing the stones to fly and strike against their tents. The ropes of the tents were breaking, and the animals were dying. I found Abu-Sufyaan, the

Commander in-Chief of the enemy forces, sitting near the fire warming himself. I thought of finishing him off. I had taken out an arrow from my quiver and placed it in my bow when I remembered the order of Nabi (Sallallahu Alayhi Wasallam). I put the arrow back into the quiver. Whilst I was among them, they became aware of my presence. They shouted, 'There is a spy amongst us. Each one of us should catch the hand of the person next to him.' I immediately caught the hand of a person and shouted, 'Who are you?' He said, 'Subhanallah! You do not know me. I am so and so.' I then returned to my camp. While I was on my way back, I met twenty horsemen with turbans on their heads. They said to me, 'Tell your master that Allah Ta'ala has dealt with his enemy and that he has nothing to worry about now.' When I reached my camp, I found Nabi (Sallallahu Alayhi Wasallam) saying his Salaah with a small shawl around him. Whenever he faced any difficulty, he immediately turned towards Salaah. When he had finished, I reported to him that I had seen in the enemy camp. When I reported how I escaped their 'search for the spy', I could see his beautiful teeth shining.[1]

There are few lessons from the the managerial point of view in the story. First the circumstances of the situation. The prophet (ﷺ) was demonstrating his bravery in the odd conditions as a manager. The quotation informs us that the prophet (ﷺ) had assigned authority to one of his companions. Consequently, it became a responsibility for the companion to accomplish the task. He did it successfully and presented the story of his journey (performance) of the enemy lines because he was accountable for it.

Line and staff authority

Line authority "refers to the formal power that a member is given to manage and make decisions about other people and resources lower than the chain of command" (Dyck and Neubert, 2009). And "staff authority refers to the formal power a member is given to provide advice and support" (Ibid, p.302). The prophet (ﷺ) had the principal line authority but he used to delegate to his companions. "Delegation is the process of giving authority to a person or group to make

---

[1] Kandhelvi, 2012.

decisions in a specified sphere of activity". (Ibid, p.302). He delegated staff authority to the leaders of migrations to Abyssinia: Usman (رضي الله عنه) and Jaffer (رضي الله عنه). Jaffer (رضي الله عنه) was a magical speaker; he demonstrated it to the king of Abyssinia and won his heart for the protection of Muslims.

Chain of support/command

Ensure orderly deference i.e. clear organisation structure, who is responsible to whom so that he can seek help and advice.

The Muslim army was divided at the conquering of Makkah into many teams which were under the control of the prophet (ﷺ). It was subdivided into many battalions each of which was headed by a leader. These were responsible for their units and suppose to report the prophet (ﷺ). On another occasion, the caravan of the prophet (ﷺ) was on a journey. It was decided to cook food over there; the prophet (ﷺ) assigned sub-tasks to everyone and assumed himself to collect firewood.

Mainstream management ensures senior managers must make decisions. In this connection Islam emphasises the importance of Ameer, the manager or ruler Narrated Abu Huraira (رضي الله عنه), Allah's Messenger (ﷺ) said,

"<u>Whoever obeys me, obeys Allah, and whoever disobeys me, disobeys Allah, and whoever obeys the ruler I appoint, obeys me, and whoever disobeys him, disobeys me.</u>" [Al-Bukhari, Volume 9, Book 89, Hadith Number 251]. He decides and assumes its responsibility. Allah, the exalted commands to the nearest effect that whenever you decide than trust Allah, the exalted.[1] The prophet (ﷺ) was making decisions or to whom he assigned it. The prophet (ﷺ) was leading salah, but he also commanded Abu Bakker (رضي الله عنه) to do it. Abu Bakker (رضي الله عنه) also lead the hajj expedition before the prophet's (ﷺ) last pilgrim.

Usman (رضي الله عنه) was appointed as the leader of the first ever migrants in the path of Allah (سبحانه و تعالى) to Abyssinia. Molana Zakerya Kandhelvi writes,[2]

> The series of persecutions started late in the fourth year of Prophethood, slowly at first, but steadily accelerated and worsened day by day and month by

---

[1] It was by the mercy of Allah that thou wast lenient with them (O Muhammad), for if thou hadst been stern and fierce of heart they would have dispersed from round about thee. So, pardon them and ask forgiveness for them and consult with them upon the conduct of affairs. And when thou art resolved, then put thy trust in Allah. Lo! Allah loveth those who put their trust (in Him). (Al-e-Imran: 159)

[2] Kandhelvi, 2012.

month until the situation got so extremely grave and no longer tolerable in the middle of the fifth year, that the Muslims began to seriously think of feasible ways liable to avert the painful tortures meted out to them ...

The Prophet (ﷺ) had already known that Ashamah Negus, king of Abyssinia (Ethiopia), was a fair ruler who would not wrong any of his subordinates, so he permitted some of his followers to seek asylum there in Abyssinia (Ethiopia). In Rajab of the fifth year of Prophet (ﷺ)hood, a group of twelve men and four women left for Abyssinia (Ethiopia). Among the emigrants were 'Uthman bin 'Affan and his wife Ruqaiyah (the daughter of the Prophet (ﷺ). With respect to these two emigrants, the Prophet (ﷺ) said: "They are the first people to migrate in the cause of All? after Abraham and Lot [AS]." They sneaked out of Makkah under the heavy curtain of a dark night and headed for the sea where two boats happened to be sailing for Abyssinia (Ethiopia), their destination. News of their intended departure reached the ears of Quraish, so some men were despatched in their pursuit, but the believers had already left

Shuaibah Port towards their secure haven where they were received warmly and accorded due hospitality.

In this way, the prophet (ﷺ) established the chain of command on various occasions.

Harmony among members

Ensure that all members work together harmoniously. It involves clarification of complementary jobs and or similar tasks. Since all Muslims was working as a team for the cause of Islam therefore, development of harmony among themselves was necessary. The prophet (ﷺ) did it in the first instance after arriving at Madinah. It was known as the creation of brotherhood. In management jargon, it was the creation of a harmonious environment for working together. It was one of the major tasks of the prophet (ﷺ) which produced enormous results. The prophet (ﷺ) used to clarify sub-tasks. He deputed Hozaifa (رضي الله عنه) to visit the opposition lines to know what they were doing. He advised the companion that does not involve in anything other than watching/observing the situation.[1]

---

[1] Kandhelvi, 2012.

Treatment of subordinates

Multiteam managers ensure treatment of every member with respect and dignity. As a prophet (ﷺ) the prophet (ﷺ) loved to his followers but as boss, the story of Zaid bin Harsa (رضي الله عنه) was famous. In the words of Molana Muhammad Zakria Kandehlvi,

Before Islam, Zaid (رضي الله عنه) was once traveling in a caravan with his mother, going to her father's town, when the Qais attacked the caravan. They took Zaid (رضي الله عنه) as a slave and sold him in Makkah Mukarramah. Hakim bin Hazam bought him for his aunt Khadijah (رضي الله عنها), who offered him as a present to Nabi (Sallallahu Alayhi Wasallam) at the time of her marriage with him. Zaid's (رضي الله عنه) father was in great grief at the loss of his son. He roamed about in search of him, mourning his separation in the following heart-breaking verses:

> "I weep in memory of Zaid, while I know not whether he is alive (to be hoped for) or finished by death." "O! Zaid, By Allah, I have no knowledge, whether you are killed on soft soil or on a rock." "Ah, I wish I knew whether you would ever come back to me, for that is the only desire I

am living for." "I remember Zaid when the sun rises in the East. I remember him when the rain comes from the clouds." "The blowing wind makes stronger the fire of his memory. Alas, my grief and suffering are very long." "I shall run my swift camels in search of him. I shall search for him around the universe." "The camels may get tired, but I shall not rest, until I die, for death is the end of every hope." "I shall still command my sons and such and such people, to keep searching for Zaid even after my death."

Some people of his family happened to meet Zaid (رضي الله عنه) during their journey to Makkah Mukarramah. They told him the story of his father's grief and pain and read to him the poems which he sang for Zaid. Zaid (رضي الله عنه) sent a letter to his father through these people. The letter consisted of three poems addressed to his father telling him that he was quite well and happy with his noble master. When the people went back, they informed his father of his location and delivered Zaid's (رضي الله عنه) message to him. On receiving the letter, his father and his uncle left for Makkah Mukarramah with sufficient money to buy Zaid (رضي الله عنه). When they came to Nabi (Sallallahu Alayhi Wasallam) they said: "O, son of Haashim and the chief of Quraish. You are living in the Haram and the neighbour of Allah Ta'ala. You are known for freeing the prisoners and feeding the hungry. We have come to you requesting for our son. Accept the ransom money for Zaid and set him free. We are willing to pay even more than the ransom money. Please, show mercy and be kind to us." Nabi (Sallallahu Alayhi Wasallam) asked: "What do you wish to do with Zaid?" Zaid's father replied: "We want to take him back home with us." "Is that all?" asked Nabi (Sallallahu Alayhi Wasallam) "All right, then call Zaid and ask him. If he wishes to go with you, I shall let him go without taking any money, but I shall not send him if he doesn't want to go." Zaid's father replied: "You have shown us more favour than we deserve. We most gladly agree to what you say." Zaid (رضي الله عنه) was sent for. When he came, Nabi (Sallallahu Alayhi Wasallam) asked Zaid (رضي الله عنه): "Do you know these men? Zaid (رضي الله عنه) replied: "Yes, I know them. This is my father and that is my uncle." www.islamicbulletin.org Stories of the Sahaabah (Radiyallahu Anhum) 111 Nabi (Sallallahu Alayhi Wasallam) then said: "And you know me too. They have come to take you back to your home. You have my full permission to go with them. If, on the other hand, you chose to stay on with me, you may do so." Zaid

(رضي الله عنه) replied: "How can I prefer anybody else to you? You are everybody for me, including my father and my uncle." Zaid's father and uncle were surprised and said: "O, Zaid! Do you prefer to be a slave? How can you leave your own father, uncle, and other members of your family, and remain a slave?" Zaid (رضي الله عنه) replied: "Verily, I have seen something in my master that makes me prefer him to everybody else in the world." On this, Nabi (Sallallahu Alayhi Wasallam) took Zaid (رضي الله عنه) in his lap and said: "From today, I adopt Zaid as my son." The father and uncle were quite satisfied with the situation and gladly left Zaid (رضي الله عنه) with Nabi (Sallallahu Alayhi Wasallam) and returned without him.

Zaid (رضي الله عنه) was only a child at that time. His preferring to remain a slave and refusing to go with his own father, giving up his home and family, shows his great love for Nabi (Sallallahu Alayhi Wasallam).

The other side of the story was more important; Zaid (رضي الله عنه) preferred to stay with the prophet (ﷺ) as a slave rather than to become a free person in his family. It tells us the love and affection of the prophet (ﷺ) for his subordinates.

And pounder (ﷺ) over the words of Ans (رضي الله عنه) who a slave of the prophet (ﷺ) was. Anas said, "I did not touch any silk brocade nor silk softer than the palm of the Messenger of Allah (ﷺ), may Allah bless him and grant him peace. I did not smell any scent sweeter than the scent of the Messenger of Allah (ﷺ). <u>I served the Messenger of Allah (ﷺ), may Allah bless him and grant him peace, for ten years and he never said to me, 'Uff' (disappointment, or sadness) nor did he say about anything I had done, 'Why did you do that?' nor about anything I had not done, 'Why did you not do that?'"</u> [Al-Bukhari & Muslim, Riyadus-Saliheen, Hadith Number 622, p. 541].

The treatment of the prophet (ﷺ) was with the slave who was not employees who work as a free person. He can leave the organisation when he does not like the employer. It may be due to financial issues or ill-treatment.

2 Organisation structure

Introduction

Manager supposed to utilise the resources in such a manner that produces the maximum possible outcome. The concept of productivity emerged in management literature to show the efficiency of resources. [1] One of a method to gain efficiency is to divide resources in a manner where they give maximum efficiency. For example, it is against this concept that two

---

[1] Online Business Dictionary defines it as, "A measure of the efficiency of a person, machine, factory, system, etc., in converting inputs into useful outputs.
Productivity is computed by dividing average output per period by the total costs incurred or resources (capital, energy, material, personnel) consumed in that period. Productivity is a critical determinant of cost efficiency."

drivers are appointed to drive a single delivery van. Alternatively, managers must generate constructive interaction.[1] This chapter deals with the way managers divide their human resources to get better productivity and constructive collaboration. We will examine the strategy of the prophet (ﷺ) in this regard.

Departmentalisation

Mainstream managers also create various departments to divide the organisation's resources and human capital. It ensures harmony among the interacting workforces. The magnitude of work was small in Makkah but it increased many folds in Madinah. It created the need for departmentalisation. The prophet (ﷺ) introduced many departments. Department of defence, education and finance were some of them.

---

[1] A state in which two or more things work together in a particularly fruitful way that produces an effect greater than the sum of their individual effects. Expressed also as "the whole is greater than the sum of its parts."

http://www.businessdictionary.com/definition/synergy.html

Department of defence

The defence was open to everyone because military training was part of the life of every male at that time. Every person used to learn how to fight a war i.e. using sward, protecting opponent attack through the shield, arrow shooting etc. others are discussed in the following paragraphs.

It was also the responsibility of everyone to keep his weapons. Nevertheless, many weapons used to break during battles. The state was providing replacements.

The prophet (ﷺ) awarded a sward to Abu Dojanah (رضي الله عنه). In the words of Mobarikpuri,

To wage and inflame his Companions and to steadfast in the fight, he took a sharp sword, held it in his hand and called out unto his companions and said: "Who is ready to take this sword and give it its proper due?" Many a man set out to take it. Some of them were 'Ali bin Abi Talib (رضي الله عنه), Az-Zubair bin Al- 'Awwam (رضي الله عنه) and 'Umar bin Al-Khattab (رضي الله عنه). But it was granted to none. Abu Dujana and (رضي الله عنه) Sammak bin Kharsha (رضي الله عنه) inquired: "O Messenger of Allâh, what is its price?" The Prophet (ﷺ) (ﷺ) said: "It is to strike the enemy's faces with it until it was bent." So,

Abu Dujana (رضي الله عنه) said: "O Messenger of Allâh I will take it for that price." and he was given the sword.

The department was necessary because the prophet (ﷺ) was forced to defend himself and his followers many times.

Departments of Education and Finance

The department of education was set up in the masjid. There was a raised platform for it called Suffah. Hazrat Shaikh writes, "The people of Suffah were living in Nabi (Sallallahu Alayhi Wasallam) Musjid. They had no regular source of income. They were the guests of Nabi (Sallallahu Alayhi Wasallam), who gave them Sadaqah and shared with them the gifts that he received. Abu Hurairah (رضي الله عنه) was one of them."

Ashab-e-Sufa were dedicated people for learning and teaching. In other words, it was the department of education of the time. Abu Huraira was one the noteworthy student of it who is responsible for more than 5,000 sayings (Ahadith) of the prophet (ﷺ).

The department of finance was established when the command of Zakat was revealed. Officers were appointed to collect it and it was distributed among poor and needy individuals and families.

Multi-stream management encourages participation as Dyck and Neubert conceived. It involves creating a sense of mutuality which gives "stakeholders a voice in how the organisation is managed and how jobs are performed" (Dyck and Neubert:2009). The prophet (ﷺ) had established a shoorah or consultation group which was responsible for making important decisions. Allah, the exalted has also commended for the consultation (Al-e-Imraan: 159). However, everyone was free to put forward any suggestions for any issue. The prophet (ﷺ) was inviting conversation after fajr salah on daily basis.[1]

Span of control

The span of control is the ratio of manager to his subordinates at various levels of an organisation.

The prophet (ﷺ) had determined the span of control; consider the following quotation in connection with the war of Trench.

The Messenger of Allâh (ﷺ) summoned a high advisory board and conducted a careful

---

[1] Siddiqi p. 109.

discussion of a plan to defend Madinah. After a lengthy talk between military leaders and people possessed of sound advice, it was agreed, on the proposal of an honourable Companion, Salman Al-Farisi, to dig trenches as defensive lines. The Muslims, with the Prophet (ﷺ), encouraging, helping, and reminding them of the reward in the Hereafter, ﷺ, at their head, most actively and diligently started to build a trench around Madinah. Severe hunger, starvation, could not dissuade or discourage them from achieving their desperately sought objective. Salman said: O Messenger of Allâh! (ﷺ) When the siege was to lay to us in Persia, we used to dig trenches to defend ourselves. It was really an unprecedented wise plan. The Messenger of Allâh (ﷺ) hurriedly gave orders to implement the plan. Forty yards was allocated to each group of ten to dig. Sahl bin Sa'd (رضي الله عنه) said: We were in the company of the Messenger of Allâh (ﷺ), the men used to dig, and we evacuate the earth on our backs.

It suggests that teams of tens were set up to accomplish the task. And it is not obvious whether the prophet (ﷺ) had appointed any head of these teams which implies that the prophet (ﷺ) was heading them. According to scholars, the number of personnel in the expedition was 3,000; thus, there were 300 teams. If we assume that the prophet (ﷺ) had appointed a head for each of the teams, then there were 300 heads of the teams. The prophet

(ﷺ) was managing/controlling himself these teams.

Thus, we can learn the managerial concept of span of control. It means "the number of members a given manager has authority over"[1] The discussion suggests that the span of control was 1 to 300; the prophet (ﷺ) head of the teams was reporting to the prophet (ﷺ). At team level, the span of control was 1 to 10 because a head was managing ten personnel.

Organisation structure

When we examine the organisation structure of the prophet (ﷺ) which he had utilised at different times, it suggests that he organised his activities on the basis of flat structure. He managed the day-to-day matters using his shoorah or a small cabinet. Prominent companions were the members of it. For example, the opinion of Abu Bakker (رضي الله عنه) and Umer (رضي الله عنه) were on the record while the decision about the prisoners of war was decided. In addition, the quotation in the above section describes that the prophet (ﷺ) had summand a meeting of the advisory board to decide about the strategy of the war of trench.

---

[1] Dyck and Neubert, 2009, p. 302.

He sent troops to Mota under the leadership of one person and said to the nearest effect that if he happened to martyr another person shall be the leader. He nominated four persons in this way. Look at the story in the words of Shaikhul Hadith Molana Muhammad Zakarya (Rahmatullah alyhe),

Of the messengers that Nabi (Sallallahu Alayhi Wasallam) sent to different kings, inviting them to Islam, one was sent to the King of Busra through Hadhrat Haris bin Umair Azdi (رضي الله عنه). When Hadhrat Haris (رضي الله عنه) reached Moota, he was killed by Sharjeel Ghassani, one of the governors of Caesar. The murder of the envoy (messenger) was against all laws.

Nabi (Sallallahu Alayhi Wasallam) was naturally very much upset when the news reached him. He collected an army, 3 000-strong in number, to advance against the enemy. Nabi (Sallallahu Alayhi Wasallam) said, "Hadhrat Zaid bin Harithah (رضي الله عنه) will command the army, If Zaid (رضي الله عنه) is killed, then Ja'far bin Abi Talib (رضي الله عنه) will be your Amir and if he is also martyred, then Abdullah bin Rawahah (رضي الله عنه) will take the command. If he also dies, then you can select a commander from among yourselves."

He had officially appointed the deputies of the leader. It implies that there was one leader only at a time. In management terms, it suggests that the layer of management was one i.e. leader and his subordinates.

The prophet (ﷺ) has appointed a team of two.[1] While performing slat two persons should do in the congregation: one leader another follower. It suggests that the principle was equally good for other matters. He has organized the army brigades based on tribes. The tribal leader used to be the head of his troops. The number (the span of control) was not determined because it varies according to the strength of the tribe.

Refer to chart 1 below, the prophet (ﷺ) was directly managing hundreds of teams. In managerial terms, it was a flat or short structure. When managers have many subordinates reporting to him it is known as wide span. It reduces the number of hierarchical layers. It is one of the popular structures in contemporary management practices. Claver-Cortés (2007) summarises the advantages of the flat structure as, "In general terms, the results show that these companies adopt

---

[1] Narrated by Abu Musa, That the Prophet (ﷺ) sent him and sent Mu'adh after him (as rulers to Yemen). [Al-Bukhari, Volume 9, Book 89, Hadith Number 270]

flexible, increasingly flat organizational forms with fewer hierarchical levels which not only allow but also encourage communication and teamwork among staff members so that everybody can interact more easily. This makes it possible for employees to take better advantage of their competencies, generating organizational routines and increasing the value of their contributions thanks to the freedom of action they are given."[1]

When we look at the second chart, it implies the prophet (ﷺ) had appointed heads for each of the teams and they were under the control of the prophet (ﷺ).

---

[1] Enrique Claver-Cortés, Patrocinio Zaragoza-Sáez, Eva Pertusa-Ortega, (2007) "Organizational structure features supporting knowledge management processes", Journal of Knowledge Management, Vol. 11 Issue: 4, pp.45-57, https://doi.org/10.1108/13673270710762701

Figure 1 Organisation chart 1

Figure 2 Organisation Chart 2

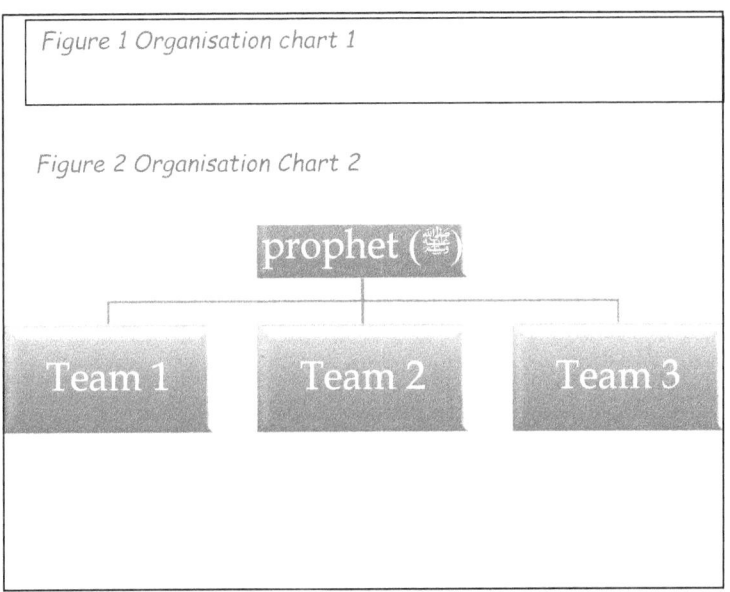

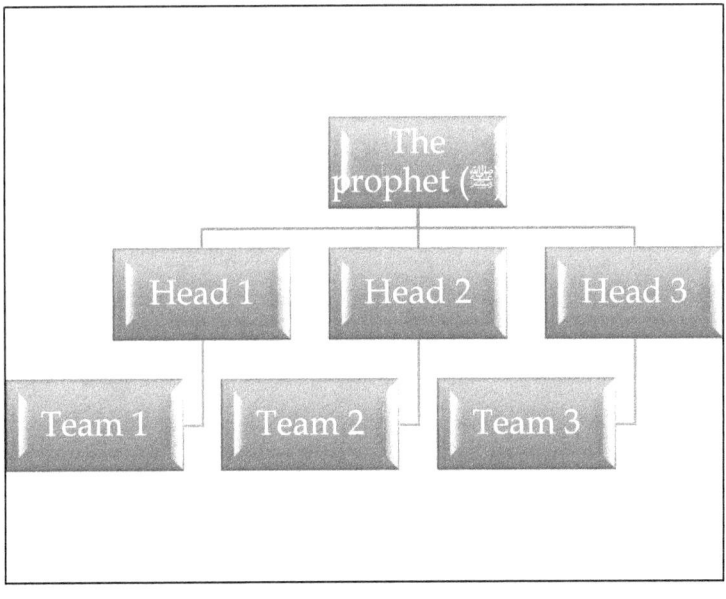

3 Resource allocation

Introduction

A manger uses resources of his organisation to maximise the outcome. We believe the resources are scare and their prudent application increases the profitability of the factors apply for generating revenue. The prophet (ﷺ) had extremely limited resources on his disposal for the new state in Madinah. He financed major projects of his time with the public contribution. However, he had utilised other resources effectively and efficiently. Some glimpses of his approach were identified from his biography.

Allocation of resources

As for as resource deployment was concerned one camel was allocated for eighteen persons at the occasion of Tabuk expedition. Mobarikpuri states,

> "despite all the gifts of wealth and mounts the army was not perfectly equipped. The

shortage of provisions and mounts was so serious that eighteen men mounted one camel alternatively. As for provisions, members of the army at times had to eat the leaves of trees till their lips got swollen. Some others had to slaughter camels — though they were so dear — so that they could drink the water of their stomach; that is why that army was called "The army of distress"."[1]

However, at the time of Hijrah, the prophet (ﷺ) and Abu Bakker (رضي الله عنه) were riding on separate she camels. It means that it depends upon the availability of resources and requirements of any endeavour.

According to Schmitz "Organizing is the function of management that involves developing an organizational structure and allocating human resources to ensure the accomplishment of objectives. The structure of the organization is the framework within which the effort is coordinated." It implies that at higher level managers should decide to achieve the objective of the organisation. It may be worthwhile to note that in the Makken era (about 13 years of his efforts) there was not a formal organisation. The prophet (ﷺ) was alone

---

[1] Mobarikpuri, P. 584.

with some companions; he was making most of the collective efforts. For example, he went to Taif alone with his slave which was one of the major campaigns he had undertaken. He also sent two groups to Abyssinia and appointed a leader for both.

However, the prophet (ﷺ) planned and implemented many military campaigns and non-military projects in Madinah. He organised his team wisely to achieve his objective. He managed the first Muslim state of Madinah; he had a team of four advisors (they became caliphs later one after another). He had also general council type team of advisors known as majlas-e-shoorah (See above).

When a formal organisation was set up in Madinah the prophet (ﷺ) had introduced organisational structure. There were a couple of teams leaders at the conquer of Makkah. He had divided the army into four divisions. [1]

The leaders of the tribes were leading their groups in most of the cases. However, Khalid (رضي الله عنه) was leading a special division before entering the city.

The prophet (ﷺ) had allocated a portion of 10 yards to ten persons to dig the trench in the

---

[1] Lings, p. 297.

third major armed encounter with Quraysh.[1] Lings said he had allocated each section of his community to do the job. But he did not define the composition of the section. Many a scholar reported the former view.

Another crucial step was taken to coordinate the affairs of the people of Madinah when 12 leaders were appointed at the occasion of the treaty of Mina. Three of them were selected from Khizraj and nine of Aws. Both were prominent tribes of Madinah who embraced Islam during hajj.

It suggests that the prophet (ﷺ) had organised his human resources successfully. The organising strategy was successful because it had achieved its objectives.

The prophet (ﷺ) had applied a flat structure; the tribal leaders were supposed to report to the prophet (ﷺ) implicitly. There was no head or chiefs of 9 or 3 chieftains of the tribes. In the case of Makkah instance, all the tribes were leading their groups for entering the city; the prophet (ﷺ) had divided the entire army into three battalions.[2] He instructed the heads to report to the prophet (ﷺ) i.e. to join

---

[1] Siddiqi, p. 459.
[2] According to Lings the number of battalions were four.

him at a given place. At the occasion of digging the trench, he assigned ten personnel a job.

The flat structure has been a recent approach famous for efficiency and fewer levels. The proponents argue that it enables senior managers to be close to customers. Consequently, the customer can access them easily. It enhances the relationship between them to achieve greater efficiency which could save cost.

Individuals and Teams

Organizational behaviour theory examines humans as an individual, in a group, and in organizational perspective. The purpose is to look at people how they perform as an individual employee and as a member of a group or more specifically a team. Weather he works with honesty by utilizing his full potential in the absence of a supervisor or otherwise. How he looks after the resources assigned to him; does he use them for organizational benefits or for personal gains? Under performance, bribe, deception and so on lie under the broader term dishonesty. When the same person becomes a member of a team, how does he cooperate with other members? Whether he emphasizes his viewpoint or also entertains the opinions of other teammates. And what is his role in the organization? Personal qualities and character play a significant role for working in teams and working for the organization.

Islam emphasizes the personal characteristics such as straightforwardness, honesty, sincerity, truthful dealing, sympathy, sacrifice for others, and respect for everyone and so on. Fear of Allah (سبحانه و تعالى), the awareness of accountability in the Hereafter, knowledge of fundamentals, adaptation of Sunnah ways in one's life is a pillar of Islamic management. The Prophet (ﷺ) has inculcated these characteristics in the lives of his sahabah (رضي الله عنه).

Team formation

An opportunity knocked on the door of the prophet (ﷺ) when he was elected the mediator for the installation of the Black Stone. He formed the most productive and plausible team. The participants were heads of the tribes or clans of Quraysh. His way of implementing the plan was democratic and pragmatic. He had also asserted his position being a leader of the project. The participants carried the Black Stone and he fixed at the right place.

The prophet (ﷺ) deputed a team for Abyssinia. There were a blend of male and female, young and mature people. The leader was a prominent figure of Quraysh in the first expedition, Usman bin Affan (رضي الله عنه). The team was smaller than the subsequent one. The size was small because it was a test case, a pilot initiative. Success could lead to rolling out the project.

The second campaign was large, and the leader was the son of Abu Talib, a well-known personality of the Arab land. Jaffer bin Abu Talib (رضي الله عنه) represented the cause of Islam in such a way that the senior figures of the king's cabinet were compelled to shed tears in response to his compelling speech. The king's verdict was in favour of the travellers. Thus, the choice of the leader was right. Narrated by Abu Musa, that the Prophet (ﷺ) sent him and sent Mu'adh after him (as rulers to Yemen). [Al-Bukhari, Volume 9, Book 89, Hadith Number 270]

It suggests his calibre of team formation. He managed the team in a successful manner in rest of his life. The prophet (ﷺ) also formed a team to govern Yemen.[1] It was unusual at the time because the head of the state was a single individual. The prophet (ﷺ) laid down the

---

[1] Narrated by Abu Musa, That the Prophet (ﷺ) sent him and sent Mu'adh after him (as rulers to Yemen). [Al-Bukhari, Volume 9, Book 89, Hadith Number 270]

foundation of power share. He sent a team consists of a single member to Madinah prior to his migration to the city for the propagation of his message (his product in contemporary terms). In the words of Kandhelvi,

> Hadhrat Urwa bin Zubayr (رضي الله عنه) narrates that when the Ansaar heard what Rasulullaah (ﷺ) had to say, became convinced and completely satisfied with his message, they believed in him and professed their Imaan. They, therefore, became one of the vehicles of good (for mankind at large) and returned to their people after promising to meet Rasulullaah (ﷺ) the following Hajj season. They then sent a message to Rasulullaah (ﷺ) requesting him to send someone to them who would call people towards the Book of Allaah because this would cause people to accept more readily.
>
> Rasulullaah (ﷺ) therefore sent Hadhrat Mus'ab bin Umayr (رضي الله عنه), who belonged to the Banu Abdud Daar tribe. He stayed among the Banu Ghanam tribe with Hadhrat As'ad bin Zuraarah (رضي الله عنه). There he taught them the sayings of Rasulullaah (ﷺ) and recited the Qur'aan to them. Later, Hadhrat Mus'ab bin Umayr (رضي الله عنه) continued his Da'wah while

staying with Hadhrat Sa'd bin Mu'aadh (رضي الله عنه). Allaah guided people at his hands until there was scarcely a home of the Ansaar that did not have Muslims in it. Even the leaders of the Ansaar accepted Islaam, including Hadhrat Arnr bin Jamooh (رضي الله عنه). The idols of the Ansaar were broken and Hadhrat Mus'ab bin Umayr (رضي الله عنه) returned to Rasulullaah (ﷺ) with the title of "Al Muqri" ("The Mentor").

There were many grounds for it. The person was previously a well-off individual. He was young and enthusiastic. His performance was outstanding. He worked hard and paved way for roll out of Islam in the area. The prophet (ﷺ) had also selected Usman (رضي الله عنه) as a delegate at the occasion of Hodabia. Usman (رضي الله عنه) was a respectable personality, soft hearted and well-known businessman. His loyalty was proverbial on top of other qualities. Quraysh offered him tawaaf (take seven circles around the Kabah) but he refused to do it without the prophet (ﷺ).

Look at the strategy of the prophet (ﷺ) to utilise the human resources he had in his disposal. A young and energetic person was selected for

Dawah in Madinah who worked untiringly. He laid down the foundations for the prophet (ﷺ) to join him forever in the new dwellings.

While the prophet (ﷺ) sent an experienced and respected person for negotiation with Quraysh at an occasion which could spark the flam of the battle between the competing parties. He was also a loyal member of his strategic team and a close relative. He was Usman (رضي الله عنه) who was also selected for the leadership of first ever migration of Muslims to Abyssinia.

4 Communication

Introduction

Communication is a part of organisation strategy as per some contemporary scholars.[1] It is the interpersonal transfer of information and understanding (Kreitner, 2009). A survey of 133 executives suggests that communication is the most desired management skill. The prophet (ﷺ) had communicated the message of Allah, the exalted in the first instance. His job was to receive the contents and convey to the companions without any change. He was "ameen", the honest, in terms of all occupations. His character was built in line with future responsibilities. One of them was communication. The holy Quran was revealed gradually; therefore, it was recorded to preserve it for future generations. He was also explaining it practically and verbally. It was

---

[1] Kreitner, p. 296-331.

known as "hadith". The companions were also learning them by heart. The scholars compiled them later. The prophet (ﷺ) applied the carrot and stick strategy. Good news for the obedience of Allah, the exalted and punishment for defaulters.

He has applied many contemporary communication strategies. Kreitner enumerated five of them.[1] For instance, he had applied the Spray & Pray strategy. It implies he conveyed information to his community. Under the strategy, managers assume that more is better, but nothing was extra. All were necessary. However, some time he was repeating a particular viewpoint to enhance understanding.

Channels of communication

Since he was the prophet (ﷺ) of the exalted, thus he was receiving the instructions from Him through the angle and disseminated to his nation. Another channel was downwards to either people or political leaders. When Hazrat Ka'b's (رضي الله عنه) reprimand ended, the prophet (ﷺ) sent one of his companions to inform him. It implies that human channel was available, and he used it frequently. The voice of some people was very lauded which could reach

---

[1] P. 305.

miles away. It was possible because there was no noise of machines. Such "high volume" people were functioning as technology as laud speakers are doing these days.

Table 1 The channels of communication			
		⟶	
Allah (سبحانه و تعالى)	Angle	The prophet (ﷺ)	Companions
	The prophet (ﷺ)	Companions	Public/leaders of other countries
		The prophet (ﷺ)	Companions/others

The absence of technology did not hinder the flow of information. The support of his Creator was with him. Allah, the exalted, used to provide secret information to him. At the occasion of conquering of Makkah, the prophet (ﷺ) wanted to keep the mission in camera for which he adopted a high-level system of secrecy. But one of his companions sent a letter to his family about the intentions of Muslims. The prophet (ﷺ) was informed through the Divine sources about the letter. He sent a team to collect it from the person who was carrying it towards its destination.

The fastest mode of communication was the horse-riders. They used to transmit verbal and written information. The prophet (ﷺ) had used written sources to communicate with tribal leaders and heads of states. Although education was not common letters were in practice.

Written communication

Since it was difficult for the prophet (ﷺ) or his representatives to invite tribal leaders, kings, or their governors physically, therefore, the prophet (ﷺ) had invited them through written communication. Hundreds of such letters were sent to them, the purpose was to invite them towards Islam peacefully. The campaign was successful and many of them entered the fold of Islam. Gilani comments about it as, when sultans and tribal leaders embraced Islam, the Arab was also attracted to this kind of invitation. It ended up at dominance and expansion of boundaries of the Muslim state. It was also a tactic of political pressure and source of motivation. Because the Makkans were conquered through force, but sultans were entering in the faith through letters of invitation. The new faith was entering into the non-Arab world mostly under the control of than superpowers; a new superpower was emerging. However, it was different from others in many respects. It was based upon equality instead of dominance, justice in place of oppression, conquering for worldly material instead of the promise of success in the Hereafter as well as in the temporary life of this world.

Nonverbal

It is also known as body language i.e. "communication based on facial expressions, poster, and appearance." (Kreteiner, 2009) The movements that accompany our words. It can enhance or worsen the meaning of what is being said. One or more periods of silence carry meaning. It may indicate doubt, lack of understanding or polite disagreement. However, it is associated with the cultural values related to a given geographical area. For instance, silence is considered the agreement in Pakistan. There is a proverb in the Urdu language that, silence is half agreement. The religious scholars at the time of nikah (marriage) supposed to take permission of bride who is usually housed in separate rooms or side of a marriage hall. He visits her with her close relatives. The scholars ask for verbal permission; if she remains silent, it means she has no objection.

Current research shows helpful behaviour is expressed through uncrossing legs, unclasping hands, moving close to other persons, smiling face, unfolding arms from across chest etc. When a person wanted to show that he is confident; he avoids hand-to-face gestures and head scratching, maintaining and erect stance, keeping steady eye contact and steepling fingertips below the chin. Nervousness is demonstrated through clearing throat, expelling air (such as "whew"), placing a hand over mouth while speaking and hurried cigarette smoking. Demonstrating superiority or proudness through peering over tops of eyeglasses, pointing at the finger, holding jacket lapels while speaking etc.

Let us examine them from the life of the prophet (ﷺ) to determine his management style.

Helpfulness

The compiler of the autobiography of the prophet (ﷺ) including ahadith had described the physical movements, facial expression, and his way of communication. Companions of the prophet (ﷺ) were listening very carefully and attentively whenever he talked to them. Abu Sufyan who was his opponent at that time described it as "I have never seen people love anyone as much as the companions of Muhammad loved Muhammad"[1]

---

[1] Kandhelvi, V. 1, p. 509.

Smiling face

It has reported about the prophet (ﷺ) that he had a smiley face and used to receive people with smiling face. (Bukhari) In another narration says to the nearest effect that meeting a Muslim brother with a smiling face is equivalent to charity.

Open door approach

Molana Manzoor Nomani (2009) reports that one of the companions of the prophet (ﷺ), described his cheerfulness as

> Jarir bin Abdullah (رضي الله عنه) says to the nearest effect that since I embraced Islam, it never happened that the prophet (ﷺ) had refused to welcome me and whenever he saw me, he smiled.[1]

Innovative elements

The prophet (ﷺ) added various novel elements in his communication strategy. Greetings (Aslamalycum) is the first sentence with which the prophet (ﷺ) used to start a conversation. One of his companions described his approach in the following words.

> Abu Hurayra said, "Whoever meets his brother should greet him. If a tree or wall comes between them and then he meets him, he should greet him on the other side." [Al-

---

[1] Naomani, Manzoor, p. 366

Adab Al-Mufrad 1010, In-book reference: Book 42, Hadith 47

English translation: Book 42, Hadith 1010]

Narrated Albara' bin 'Azib: Allah's Messenger ordered us to do.
seven (things): to visit the sick, to follow the funeral processions, to say *Tashmit'* to a sneezer, to help the weak, to help the oppressed ones, to propagate *As-Salim* (greeting), and to help others to fulfil their oaths (if it is not sinful). He forbade us to drink from silver utensils, to wear gold rings, to ride on silken saddles, to wear silk clothes, *Dibaj* (thick silk cloth), *Qassly* and *Istabraq* (two kinds of silk).
[Al-Bukhari, *Hadith* No. 6235]

It is an ice breaker in the first instance. Secondly, it is a supplication, through which the initiator conveys to the recipients that your property, respect, and you are safe from me. In other words, I respect all of these. Thirdly it is a value of Islamic culture. In addition, it brings mercy of Allah, the exalted. The initiator gets 10-30 rewards as described in the following saying of the prophet (ﷺ).

'Imran bin Husain (May Allah be pleased with them) reported: A man came to the Prophet (ﷺ) and said: "As-Salamu 'Alaikum (may you be safe from evil). Messenger of Allah (ﷺ) responded to his greeting and the man sat down. The Prophet (ﷺ) said, "Ten (meaning the man had earned the merit of ten good acts)." Another one came and said: "As-Salamu

'Alaikum wa Rahmatullah (may you be safe from evil, and Mercy of Allah be upon you)." Messenger of Allah (ﷺ) responded to his greeting and the man sat down. Messenger of Allah (ﷺ) said, "Twenty." A third one came and said: "As-Salamu 'Alaikum wa Rahmatullahi wa Barakatuhu (may you be safe from evil, and the Mercy of Allah and His Blessings be upon you)." Messenger of Allah (ﷺ) responded to his greeting and the man sat down. Messenger of Allah (ﷺ) said, "Thirty."[1]

Attentive listener

Whenever the prophet (ﷺ) joined a conversation, he did not start a new topic joined the ongoing conversation. He paid attention to each of the participants. If anyone asked unrelated question/subject, he postponed it until the existing topic concluded. Then used to address the issue raised during the discussion.

He remained attentive to a single person until he completes his conversation. If someone wants to say something in low tune, he bowed down his head towards him.

The prophet (ﷺ) did not interfere in the talk of a person (s). However, if something is against the basics of Islam or he did not like. He corrects it or demonstrate his uncomfortableness through facial

---

[1] Nawawi, Imam, Riyad As-Salihin, Abridged edition, (2014), Hadith 429, p. 280.

expression or leave the conversation. He did not like to talk about an important topic while standing.

Correction of mistakes

He did not nominate or pinpoint any one in a gathering or otherwise. He used to indicate a wrongdoing or advice in a compact manner. In case of any religious matter, he avoids a person or hesitates to answer his greeting. But always welcome bad people of his community. Some ahadith are examples of his management of mistakes.

1-Abu Hurayra said, "<u>A Bedouin urinated in the mosque. The people moved towards him and the Prophet (ﷺ), may Allah bless him and grant him peace, said, 'Let him be and pour a bucket or pail of water onto his urine. You were sent to make things easy and not to make them difficult.'</u>" [Muslim, Book 2, Hadith, Number 557, it is also reported by Bukhari]

2- Mu'awiya ibn al-Hakam as-Sulami said, "While I was praying with the Messenger of Allah, may Allah bless him and grant him peace, a man among the people sneezed and I said, 'May Allah show you mercy.' The people looked hard at me, and I said, 'May your parents be bereaved! Why are you looking at me?' They began to hit their hands on their thighs. Then I saw that they were trying to make me be silent, so I was silent. When the Messenger of Allah, may Allah bless him and grant him peace, had finished praying - may my father and mother be his ransom, I have never seen a better teacher before or after him - by Allah, he did not rebuke me or hit me or abuse me. He merely said, 'It is not fitting to have any speech from people in the prayer. It is the only glorification and proclaiming Allah great and reciting the Qur'an.' Or as the Messenger of Allah said. I said, 'Messenger of Allah, I was until recently in a state of pre-Islamic ignorance, but Islam has now come to us. There are still men among us who go to the soothsayers.' He said, 'Do not go to them.' I said, 'Among us, there are still men who follow omens.' He said, 'That is something which they find in their breasts. They should not influence them.'" [Muslim, Riyadus-Saliheen, Hadith Number 701][1]

---

[1] Saani, Javed Iqbal (2016) Responsibilities of Managers: Selected Ahadith, available on amazon.co.uk. (Paperback edition)

5 Case Study – The battle of Uhad

Introduction

Since the infidels received an unprecedented defeat at the hands of Muslims in Badr a year ago, therefore, they were preparing to take revenge as soon as possible. They sought the help of other tribes of the region because they knew it was not an easy task to challenge Muslims alone. Three thousand troops were equipped with state-of-the-art weaponry including 200 fighting horses and seven hundred shields. The army advanced towards Madinah in the second year of Hijrah. Let us see what strategy the prophet (ﷺ) had articulate and implemented to combat it from a managerial point of view.

The initial preparations

The prophet (ﷺ) had received a letter from his uncle Abbas (رضي الله عنه) who was examining the preparation and movements of Quraysh closely and constantly. He wrote details of what was happening in Makkah. He advised Abi bin Kaab (رضي الله عنه) to keep it secret.

The prophet (ﷺ) immediately consulted migrants and Helpers. A war was on the brink of Madinah. Everyone was ready to defend the sacred land; a small battalion was appointed to guard the prophet (ﷺ). Some troops were installed at the entrances of the city to encounter any sudden attack. A patrol was established to look after the possible entry points of the enemy around the city.

In addition, the prophet (ﷺ) had also set up an information/intelligence team to keep an eye on the movement of the enemy. The team informed him in the first week of Shawal 6 AH that the enemy troops had encamped in the outstrips of the city. He called a high-level meeting of the consulting team or shoorah to discuss the defence strategy. Two opinions emerged: to remain in the city and defend it, the second was to fight in the open space. Near about the mountain of Uhad. The prophet (ﷺ) was in favour of the former while most of the young companions were supporting the later view. The prophet (ﷺ) had selected the later one.

He led the Jummah prayer, motivated people for the battle and announced that everyone should get prepared for it. People were incredibly happy, and they gathered at the time of asr salah. The Awali team had also arrived. The prophet (ﷺ) himself dressed for the combat.

Organisation of the workforce

The prophet (ﷺ) had divided the entire army into three groups:

1. Migrants
2. The tribe of Aws
3. The tribe of Khazraj

The flag bearers were appointed; the total number of mojahadeen was 1000 including 100 shield bearers and 50 horse riders.

He appointed Ibn-e-Umm-e-Maktoom to lead the prayers in the city; in other words, he was the deputy of the prophet (ﷺ).

The Islamic army advanced towards the enemy; the prophet (ﷺ) inspected the troops. Underage participants were returned. Rafy bin Khataij was at home in arrow shooting therefore, he was allowed to join the army. Another underage

Samrah bin Jundhub was also permitted to participate. Mubarikpuri (1995) states,

> The Messenger of Allâh (ﷺ) allowed both Rafi 'bin Khadaij and Samura bin Jundub to join the army — though they were too young. The former proved to be skilful at shooting arrows; the latter wrestled the former and beat him. The admission of Rafi 'made Samura say: "I am stronger than him, I can overcome him." When the Prophet (ﷺ) (ﷺ) heard this saying, he ordered them to wrestle. They did. Samura won so he was also admitted.

The prophet (ﷺ) prayed remaining slats of the day at the spot and decided to stay there overnight. Fifty persons were appointed to look after the security of the entire camp. He moved early morning and encamped the troops near the Uhad mountain. It was a natural defence line; the enemy army was in front and the city of Madinah was behind the Makken troops.

He appointed a team of fifty archers to guard the possible entry point of the enemy. Imam Bukhari summarises the appointment.

> Narrated Al-Bara: We faced the pagans on that day (of the battle of Uhud) and the Prophet (ﷺ) placed a batch of archers (at a special place) and appointed `Abdullah (bin Jubair) as their commander and said,

"Do not leave this place; if you should see us conquering the enemy, do not leave this place, and if you should see them conquering us, do not (come to) help us," So, when we faced the enemy, they took to their heels till I saw their women running towards the mountain, lifting up their clothes from their legs, revealing their leg-bangles. The Muslims started saying, "The booty, the booty!" `Abdullah bin Jubair said, "The Prophet (ﷺ) had taken a firm promise from me not to leave this place." But his companions refused (to stay). So, when they refused (to stay there), (Allah) confused them so that they could not know where to go, and they suffered seventy casualties.[1]

If we examine the overall strategy of the prophet (ﷺ) we can say that the plan of defence was the best in the circumstances. Mubarikpuri sums up it as,

> It was a wise and carefully laid plan which revealed the genius of military leadership that the Prophet (ﷺ) (ﷺ) possessed. No other leader could have drawn a more accurate or wise plan.

---

[1] Sahih al-Bukhari, Vol. 5, Hadith 4043.

Although he approached the site later than the enemy, he managed to occupy better positions. He made the rocky mountainside to function as a shield for the army's rear and right flank. He was able, by blocking the only vulnerable gap on the side, to provide additional maximum protection for the rear as well as the left wing. For fear of defeat, and to deter the Muslims from fleeing, in which case they would fall easy prisoners in the hands of the enemy, he chose a high place for an encampment.

Moreover, a strategic site of this sort would surely inflict heavy losses on the polytheists if they thought of approaching or occupying his positions. In a further step, he reduced the enemy to a narrow scope of choice when they were cornered for encampment in geographically low positions that would avail them nothing of the benefits of any possible victory; at the same time, they would not be able to escape the pursuit of the Muslims in case victory sided with the latter. To make up for the quantitative shortage in fighting personnel, he chose a picked body of fighters to stand at the front.[1]

---

[1] P. 348.

We will analyse the plan later when we discuss the implications of the strategy.

Encouragement

The prophet (ﷺ) encouraged his companions before the game. He said, when you encounter your enemy, be brave and steadfast. He took out a new sward and announced. Who wants it? Many lions of Arab offered themselves to have the weapon to pay its due. Abu Dojanah (رضي الله عنه) asked what the right/price of the sward is, the prophet (ﷺ) replied, you fight with it until it gets bent. Abu Dojanah (رضي الله عنه) said I would make it. The tool was handed over to him, who paid his price as he promised.

The battle was in favour of Muslims in the first instance but tables were turned later when the infidels enabled to launch a flank attack. Muslims sustained heavy casualties but remained steadfast. The enemy returned to Makkah without cashing last movement's upper hand.

The prophet (ﷺ) gathered his companions and supplicate to his creator for his help and benevolence. It was part of his motivational tactics because victory or otherwise is coming from the treasures of Allah. He bestowed upon him the victory in Badr, but the loss was destined in Uhad. Both were the decisions of Allah (سبحانه و تعالى) because He wanted to test His servants in all circumstances. How they perform in happiness and what would be their reaction in distress? His pleasure is under the swords. One must show his steadfastness, perseverance, resilience, and dependence upon Him. The Muslims demonstrated these qualities and became successful in the test.

The prophet (ﷺ) continued condolence and encouragement on the way back to Madinah while meeting the relatives of martyrs. He gave glad tidings of Allah's (سبحانه و تعالى) pleasure and aboard in paradise for them as well as their heirs.

Strategic action

The prophet (ﷺ) conceptualised as a military commander and a vigilant leader that the enemy could reattack because when they would realise the undecided outcome of the encounter while they had upper hand upon Muslims. They could harvest the benefits of their efforts. Next day he ordained that the Islamic army would follow the infidels lest they come back. He announced that only early participants would accompany him. The head of hypocrites requested to join hands, but he refused. The purpose was to inform them that Muslims could live without them.

In fact, when infidels realised at the first stop towards Makkah that they had not cashed the victorious position, they decided to launch another attack on Madinah. However, the prophet (ﷺ) deputed a new Muslim Maabad bin Abi Maabad Khazai (رضي الله عنه) to discourage Abu Sufyaan for a possible reattack. He went to the infidel camp and informed them that the Muslims are following them with more headcounts. It discouraged the enemy to think about a possible reattack.

The prophet (ﷺ) marched towards Hamrah Al-Asad, about eight miles from Madinah towards Makkah to chase the enemy. The Islamic troops encamped there for three days. However, the enemies could not dare to challenge them and flew to their homes.

6 Managerial Implications

Introduction

Given the case study, we will try to extract the rule and responsibilities of the prophet (ﷺ) as a managing authority of the expedition of Uhad. Our focus would be on organising function as prevalent in contemporary management practices. Organising involves assigning tasks and creating a structure of relationship where people work to achieve their organisational goals. It includes a definition of authority structure, departmentalization, the physical layout of the facilities (or battle field) and human resources.[1] And communication system and mechanism because it was the information system of the time.[2]

---

[1] Dyck and Neubert, p.8.
[2] Kreitner, p.295

The goal of endeavour was to defend the newly born organisation i.e. the state of Madinah. In business terms, a product includes a physical artefact, service, idea, or promotion of a personality. Therefore, the organisation was offering Islam as an ideology of life or product.

The authority structure consists of the prophet (ﷺ) and the shoorah/the consulting team. Prominent companions were the members of the team such as Abu Bakr, Umer, Usman, Ali, and others. The leaders of Aws and Khazraj (Two tribes of Madinah) were also part of it. The prophet (ﷺ) had appointed Ibn-e-Umm-e-Maktoom (رضي الله عنه) as his deputy to remain in Madinah. If we examine the division of troops at the time of Uhad, we can see that the organisation structure was like the following (See Figure 3 also).

It shows the prophet (ﷺ) had decentralised the authority to the leaders of these teams. They were:

1. Mus 'ab bin 'Umair Al- 'Abdari (رضي الله عنه)

2. Usaid bin Hudair (رضي الله عنه)

3. Al-Hubab bin Al-Mundhir (رضي الله عنه)

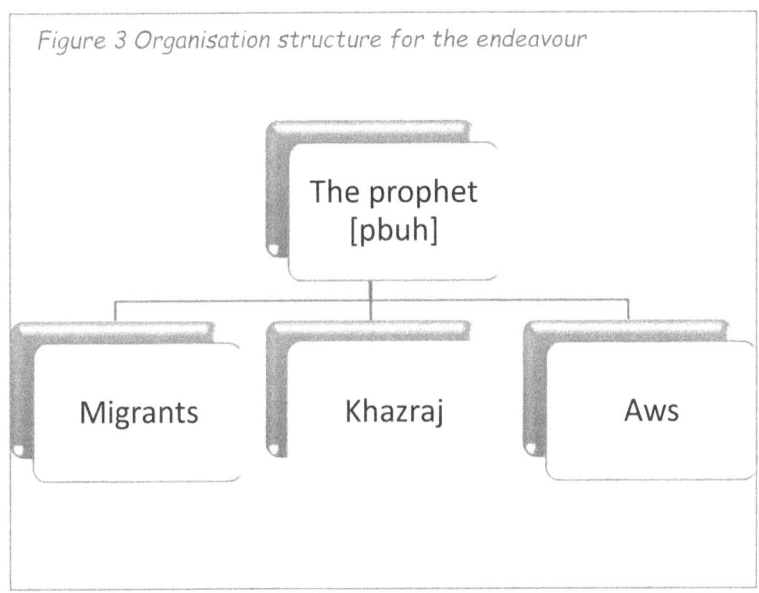

Figure 3 Organisation structure for the endeavour

Molana Shibli Naomani adds that the horse riders were under the command of Zobair bin Awwam (رضي الله عنه) and shield wearers were handed over to Hamza (رضي الله عنه), Abdullah bin Jabair (رضي الله عنه) was the commanders of fifty archers who were appointed at the strategic pass called Jabal Al-Ramadah.[1]

Definition of roles and responsibilities

It is important for the workforce to know their roles and responsibilities. The prophet (ﷺ) had assigned these to four functional departments

---

[1] Naomani and Nadvi, p. 227.

of his troops. Special emphasis was placed on the archers who supposed to guide a strategic pass. In business or management terms it was a product where the competitor could penetrate. For instance, if the organisation structure is based on geographical areas where one of the market segments is vulnerable or prone to the competitors' attention because they might be focusing upon the niche.

The prophet (ﷺ) emphasised the importance of the pass. Mabarikpuri (1995) beautifully summarises it.

> He selected fifty skilful archers that formed a squad and made them under the command of 'Abdullah bin Jubair bin An-Nu 'man Al-Ansari Al-Awsi Al-Badri (رضي الله عنه). He issued his orders to them to stay where they were — on a mountain(side) at the south bank of Qanat Al-Wadi (i.e. a canal of the valley), southeast of Muslims camp at about one hundred and fifty metres from the Islamic army. Later, this mountain was called the Mountain of Archers.
>
> The Messenger of Allâh (ﷺ) clarified the mission of this squad in words he directed to them. He said to their leader: "Drive off the horses from us by means of arrows, lest they should attack us from behind

(the rear). Whether we win the battle or lose it, stand steadily in your position and mind that we are not attacked from your side."

He further added:

> "Defend our backs! If you see our slain. Do not come to assist us; and if you see gaining grounds,
>
> do not share us."

In a version by Al-Bukhâri the Prophet (ﷺ) said:

> I "If you see us snatched into pieces by birds, do not leave this position of yours till I send for you.
>
> And if you see that we have defeated the enemy and trodden on them do not desert your position till I send for you."

With the assignment of this squad and locating it on the mountainside and the issuance of those strict military orders, the Messenger of Allâh (ﷺ) blocked the only groove that might lead the idolaters stealthily to the rear of Muslim ranks and might even enable them to encircle them in an encompassment procedure.[1]

---

[1] Mubarikpuri (1995), p. 348.

The instructions were in detail because they were extraordinarily important for the endeavour. Since the appointees left the pass, therefore, the enemy took full advantage of it. And it became the apparent reason for the heavy loss of Muslims.

The physical layout of the facilities

He then fixed the rest of force in the words of the same author, "On the right wing, he appointed Al-Mundhir bin 'Amr (رضي الله عنه). On the left, he appointed Az-Zubair bin Al- 'Awwam (رضي الله عنه) and made Al-Miqdad bin Al-Aswad (رضي الله عنه) his assistant and supporter. Az-Zubair's (رضي الله عنه) function was too steadfast in the face of Khalid bin Al-Waleed's (رضي الله عنه) horsemen. The Messenger of Allâh (ﷺ) selected the top and the most courageous group to be in the vanguard of the army. They were notable for their readiness, alertness, and bravery and estimated to be equal to thousands of men."

The plan of the prophet (ﷺ) was designed with care keeping into account all dangers and the way they could be addressed. He occupied the best possible position keeping the mountain at the back which was a natural defence. He did it after the enemy who had occupied the best position because they arrived first. The right side was also safe due to the rocks. The left wing was protected through the appointment of archers. He encamped at high grounds to have a psychological advantage over the enemy and to prevent companions to leave the battlefield in case of odd circumstances. The opponents could not capture the Islamic troops because they were at the high places. At one time when the enemy tried to advance towards the central command (where the prophet (ﷺ) was staying), the companions threw stones which worked more than arrows. It was the benefit of the geographical position the prophet (ﷺ) had selected.

At the closing moments of the battle the prophet (ﷺ) climbed on the top of the mountain which was out of the reach of the enemy. Nevertheless, Abu Sufyan, the commander-in-chief of the enemy forces, tried to approach them but the companions threw stones to them. Since Muslims were at the high ground, therefore, the infidels could not reach them and withdrew with heavy casualties. [1]

Departmentalisation

When an organisation became big so that different professionals work as per their expertise, department is created to distribute

---

[1] Naomani and Nadvi, p. 231.

the work. The prophet (︎) had created four departments for the endeavour: infantry, shield bearers, horse riders and archers (Figure 4).

Figure 4 Functional organisation structure

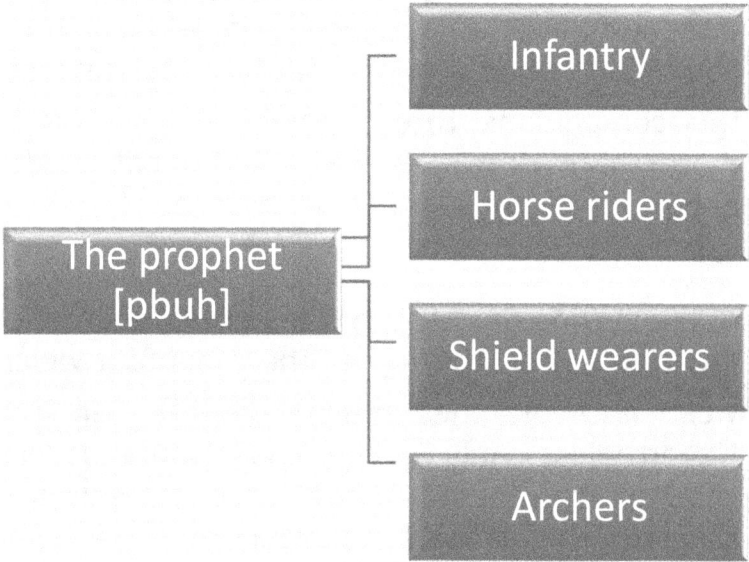

He appointed heads for each of them so that they could function effectively and efficiently. They were working directly under the command of the prophet (︎). Typically, there are five departments in the contemporary business organisations: marketing, finance, production, information services and human resources. We had already examined the importance of archers and their specific responsibility. In fact, the

Muslims were winning the war but when this squared left the pass unguarded, the enemy found an opportunity for flank attack. It caused heavy human losses to them. Everyone realised the importance of archers later. It suggests the importance of departments. All other were working well but when one of them did not function as it ought to be, the competition was almost lost to the opponents.

Human resource management

According to one estimate, the number of enemy troops was 3000. Other details of the armies are described in table 1.

Table 1 Comparison of resources

Resource	Infidels	Muslims
Camels	3,000	NA
Horses	200	50
Shields	700	100
Women	15 inspirers	Some for medical aid and provision of water to the injured

| **Troops** | 3,000 | 700 |

The numerical combat was between 1 to almost 5. Horses were 1 to 8, and shield 1 to 7. Horses were a strategic advantage at the times because one person was riding a horse, and the other was walking on the ground. The former could attack quickly and effectively upon the later. The advantages of ground troops were the shields because the attack could be stopped on it. But the Muslim army was in sever disadvantage in this aspect as well. Thus, if we look at the numbers, the infidels were in quantitative advantage. The prophet (ﷺ) had utilised his human capital in such a way that their performance was outstanding. He managed to sustain the attack and safely brought back his personnel to the garrison.

Heavy losses were due to the action of the archers. Had they not left the pass the enemy could not be able to launch a flan attack which causes casualties. However, we believe that all was from Allah (سبحانه و تعالى) who tested Muslims in either condition. He tested them in Badr after a victory while He was testing them here after losses.

Selection of personnel

One of the fundamental issues in human resource management is to pick the right people for the right job. The prophet (ﷺ) had carefully selected his troops. All people in Madinah who enabled for military service were with him. However, he had examined them at the first stop of his journey from the city to ensure that all were there. However, there were some underage boys which he returned. One of them was at home in arrow shooting, he was included in the ranks because arrows are fired from the distance which does not endanger the life of the archer under normal cases. There was another boy of his age, he was very eager to join hands with the prophet (ﷺ). He said I am stronger than the arrow shooter so I should be included. He said I can show my strength. The prophet (ﷺ) asked them to have combat with the arrow shooter. So, he got upper hand, consequently, he was permitted to remain in the serving forces.

The prophet (ﷺ) had chosen the first one based on his special skill while the other was selected for his strength. The physical strength was a skill for the battles of that time. The second feature of his human resource strategy was that he had examined every person. There was a companion who was unable to walk properly, the prophet (ﷺ) had exempted him from the military services. Thirdly, he has appointed a deputy to look after the affairs of the city and to lead the salat. It means there were other people who could pray salat i.e. they were adults. They were left to defend the city.[1] And keeping women and children in a safe place i.e. castles. Two companions were appointed to manage them.[2]

Communication strategy

Some contemporary scholars believe that communication is also a part of the 'organisation' function of managers.[3] The prophet (ﷺ) had developed a systemic communication mechanism. Let us have a look at it.

With the connection with battle, uncle of the prophet (ﷺ) was in Makkah; he was observing the activities and preparations of infidels about a revenge attack. When the troops were ready to march towards Madinah, he sent a messenger to the prophet (ﷺ) to talk about the advancement of infidel army. Abi bin Kaab (رضي الله عنه) read the letter; the prophet (ﷺ) advised

---

[1] Mobarikpuri, p. 348-49.
[2] Phalwarvi, p. 331.
[3] Kreitner, p. 296-331.

him for secrecy and called the meeting for planning the expedition.[1]

The prophet (ﷺ) had appointed Ans and Munus to keep an eye on the movement of the enemy army. They continued to update the prophet (ﷺ) about every movement of the opponents.[2] When the infidel force reached near Madinah, the prophet (ﷺ) had appointed Khabab bin Manzar (رضي الله عنه) to estimate the number of enemy personnel and equipment.[3]

The people of Madinah were also in contact with the battlefield. When Muslims sustained losses and retreated towards the mountain, reserves rushed towards their comrades. It also included the family members of the prophet (ﷺ).

The prophet (ﷺ) had kept an eye upon the opponents even after they took their way towards Makkah. He appointed a new Muslim to demotivate Abu Sufyan about a possible reattack. The judgment of the prophet (ﷺ) was correct, the enemy was trying to resume his ill-fated efforts. But with the timely managerial action, it did not happen.

---

[1] Mobarikpuri, p. 340.
[2] Razi, p. 208.
[3] Naomani and Nadvi, p. 226.

Ha has applied an innovative approach to organising the resources. The prophet (ﷺ) had positioned his troops against the mount Uhad which provided him natural defence from two sides. He had covered the third one with a special battalion. Thus, every effort had been made to plan the endeavour to win the game.

BIBLIOGRAPHY

Adair, John (2010) The Leadership of Muhammad (pbuh), New Delhi: Kogan Page India Private Limited.

Al-Bahaqi, Abi Bakker Ahmad Al-Hussain (2009) Dhalail Al-Nabuwwa, Karachi: Dharul Ishaat.

Allen, Louis A. (1958) Management and organization, New York: McGraw-Hill.

DeCenzo, David A. and Stephen P. Robbins (2010) Human Resource Management, New York: John Wiley & Sons.

Dess, Gregory G., G. T. Lumpkin, Alan B. Eisner (2006) Strategic Management: Text and Cases, New York: Irwin/McGraw-Hill.

Dyck, B and Mitchell J Neubert (2009) Principal of Management, South-Western.

Fulop, L, and S Linstead (1999) Management, A critical text, London: Macmillan.

Haimann, Theo and Raymond L. Hilgert (1972) Supervision: Concepts and Practices of Management, South-Western Publishing Company.

Hameed Ullah, M. (2006) The Prophet's (ﷺ) Establishing a State and his Succession, Beacon Books: Lahore.

Iqbal, Javed, and Muhammad Mushtaq Ahmad (2009) Planning in the Islamic Tradition: The Case of Hijrah Expedition, INSIGHTS 01(3), 37-68.

Kaandhlawi, Muhammad Zakarya (1997), Fazail-e-Amaal, Lahore: Kutibkhana Faizi.

Kaandhlawi, Muhammad Yusuf (2012), Hayatus Sahabah, Delhi: Islamic Books Services.

Koontz, Harold, and Heinz Weihrich (2006) Essentials of Management, New Delhi: Tata McGraw-Hill Education, pp. 81-84.

Kreitner, R (2009) Principal of Management, South-Western.

Lings, M M (1994) Muhammad, his life based on the earliest sources, Lahore: Suhail Academy.

Mubarakpuri, Safiur Rahman (1995) "The Sealed Nectar" (Ar-Raheeq Al-Makhtum), Lahore: Al-Maktba Alsalfia.

Nadvi, Sulaiman Hussaini (2205) Khutbat-e-Seerat, Karachi: Zam Zam Publishers.

Noamani, Shibli and Syed Solaiman Nadhvi (2004) Seeratun-Nabi, Karachi: Dharul-Ishaat.

Pea, Roy D. (2015) What Is Planning Development the Development of? Accessed: April 2015, http://web.stanford.edu/~roypea/RoyPDF%20folder/A11_Pea_82d.pdf

Phalwari, Muhammad Jaafer (1995) Peghambr-e-Insaniat, Lahore: Idara Sakafat-e-Islamia.

Razi, Muhammad Wali (1987) Hadhi-e-Alam, Dharul-Ilm: Karachi.

Robbins, Stephen, and Mary Coulter (2017) Management, New Delhi: Pearson Education.

Saani, Javed Iqbal (2017) Prophet (ﷺ) Muhammad (ﷺ) as a planning expert, London: Intellectual Capital Enterprise Limited.

Saani, Javed Iqbal (2016) Responsibilities of Managers: Selected Ahadith, available on amazon.co.uk. (Paperback edition)

Siddiqi, Naeem (1997) The Benefactor of Humanity (Mohsin-e-Insaniyat), Dehli: Markazi Matabah Islami Publishers.

Smith, Mike (2007) Fundamentals of Management, Berkshire: McGraw Hill Education.

Tiem Management Guide (2015) What is planning and why you need to plan, Accessed: April 2015, http://www.time-management-guide.com/planning.html

INDEX

A

Abu Dojanah, 59
Abu'd-Darda, XI
Abyssinia, 10, 12, 33, 37, 40
accountability, 2, 5, 36
affairs, XIII, XIX
Al-Bukhari, 11, 18
Al-Bukhâri, 67
Al-e-Imraan, 23
Allah, IX, XI, XV, XVII, XIX, XXI, 3, 7, 10, 11, 14, 15, 18, 23, 36, 50, 57, 59, 60, 72
Allah (SWT), XV, XIX, XXI
Anas, IX, 18
appointed, 5, 11, 23, 24, 27, 33, 34, 54, 55, 56, 64, 65, 68, 70, 74, 75, 86
archers, 3, 4, 56, 65, 66, 69, 70, 72
assignment, 1, 67
associate, 86
Australia, *87*
authority, 5, 9, 25, 63, 64
Aws, 55, 64

B

behaviour, 35

C

Camels, 71
case study, XXI, 63, 92

command, 1, 4, 9, 15, 23, 26, 65, 66, 69, 70
commander, 27, 56, 60, 69
communication, 28, 63, 74
companion, 9, 13, 73
coordinate, 34

D

Delegation, 9
dementalization, 63
departments, 20, 65, 70
development, 13
Dyck and Neubert, 5, 6, 9, 23, 25, 63

E

England, *86*

F

flat structure, 25, 28
forgive, XXI
forgiveness, XI, XIII, XXI

H

Hadith Number, 11, 18
hierarchical, 28
Hodabia, 5, 39
Horses, 71, 72

I

implications, XXI

infidel, 61, 74, 75
information, XVII, 54, 70
Islam, XIX, 2, 10, 13, 14, 26, 34, 36, 37, 39, 64

K

Khazraj, 55, 64
knowledge, IX, XI, *87*

L

leader, XV, XIX, 2, 4, 10, 11, 26, 27, 33, 37, 57, 60, 66

M

Madinah, 13, 20, 24, 31, 33, 34, 38, 40, 53, 54, 56, 60, 61, 64, 73, 74, 75
Makkah, 10, 12, 14, 15, 20, 33, 34, 54, 59, 61, 74, 75
management, XX, 5, 10, 13, 23, 27, 28, 32, 36, 63, 66, 71, 73, 79
Management, 77, 86, 92
Managerial, XXI
managerial action, 75
Managers, XXI, 1, 91, 92
managing, XIX
Messenger, IX, XI, *10*, *18*
Messenger of Allâh, 24, 56, 66, 67, 68
migrants, 11, 54
Migrants, 55
Molana Shibli, 65
Mota, 26
Mountain, 66
Mubarikpuri, 56, 57

Muhammad, XIII, XV, 91, 92
Muslim, 50, 51
Muslims, 4, 10, 12, 13, 24, 39, 40, 53, 57, 58, 59, 60, 61, 66, 69, 71, 72, 75

O

organisation, 2, 10, 20, 23, 31, 32, 33, 64, 66, 69, 70, 74
Organising, 1, 63
organize, 1

P

pardon, XIII
physical layout, 63
plan, 24, 36, 57, 59, 68, 79
Planning, XX
pleasure, XI, XIX
project, XVII, 37
prophet, XV, XX, 3, 5, 9, 10, 11, 13, 14, 17, 20, 23, 24, 25, 27, 31, 32, 33, 34, 36, 37, 39, 40, 53, 54, 55, 56, 57, 59, 60, 61, 63, 64, 65, 66, 68, 69, 70, 72, 73, 74, 75
Prophet, 91
Prophets, XI, XIX

R

responsibility, 1, 5, 9, 11, 70
revenue, 31
Riyadus-, 18

S

Selection of personnel, 73
Shields, 71

span of control, 24, 25, 27
strategy, 26, 34, 40, 53, 54, 57, 59, 73, 74
structure, 10, 19, 25, 27, 28, 32, 33, 34, 35, 63, 64, 66, 70
subordinates, 12, 14, 17, 27, 28

T

task, 3, 6, 9, 13, 24, 53
team, XIX, 3, 5, 13, 27, 33, 36, 37, 40, 54, 55, 56, 64
teams, 1, 2, 24, 27, 36, 64

troops, 26, 27, 53, 54, 55, 56, 61, 64, 66, 69, 71, 72, 73, 74
truthful, XIX

U

Ummah, XV

W

Will of a sick person, 49
work, 2, 3, 5, 13, 20, 63, 69
worship, XI

OTHER BOOKS BY THE AUTHOR (S)

1. Prof Dr. Javed Iqbal Saani (2018) Planning Strategy of the Prophet (ﷺ)[pbuh], Intellectual Capital Enterprise Limited, London, available on amazon (Paperback edition)
2. Prof Dr. Javed Iqbal Saani (2018) Qualities of Momins: The Quranic Perspective, Intellectual Capital Enterprise Limited, London, available on amazon (Paperback edition)
3. Prof Dr. Javed Iqbal Saani (2018) Hajj Experience: Combining Dawah and Manasiks, Intellectual Capital Enterprise Limited, London, available on amazon (Paperback edition)
4. Prof Dr. Javed Iqbal Saani (2018) Sukhn-e-Saani (The book of poetry), Intellectual Capital Enterprise Limited, London, available on amazon (Paperback edition)
5. Prof Dr. Javed Iqbal Saani (2018) Managing Your Projects, Intellectual Capital Enterprise Limited, London, available on amazon.co.uk. (Paperback edition)
6. Prof Dr. Javed Iqbal Saani (2017) Business Case Studies, Intellectual Capital Enterprise

Limited, London, available on amazon (Paperback edition)

7. Prof Dr. Javed Iqbal Saani (2017) Virtues of Sickness: Selected Ahadith, available on amazon (Paperback edition)

8. Prof Dr. Javed Iqbal Saani (2017) Prophet (ﷺ) Muhammad (ﷺ) as a planning expert, available on amazon (Paperback edition)

9. Prof Dr Javed Iqbal Saani (2017) Muhammad (ﷺ): His Trials & Tribulations, available on amazon (Paperback edition)

10. Prof Dr. Javed Iqbal Saani (2017) Sales and Marketing: Selected Ahadith, available on amazon.co.uk. (Paperback edition)

11. Prof Dr. Prof Dr. Javed Iqbal Saani (2016) Research Proposals: Contents & Exemplars, available on amazon.co.uk. (Paperback edition)

12. Prof Dr. Javed Iqbal Saani (2016) Responsibilities of Managers: Selected Ahadith, available on amazon.co.uk. (Paperback edition)

13. Prof Dr. Javed Iqbal Saani (2016) Experience: The Journey of My Life, available on amazon.co.uk. (Paperback edition)

14. Prof Dr. Javed Iqbal Saani (2012) Understanding Information Systems, Manchester: GRaASS.

15. Prof Dr Javed Iqbal Saani (2011) Digital Divide in South Asia ISBN: 9789699578120.
16. Prof Dr. Javed Iqbal Saani and Muhammad Rafi Khattak (2011) Managing Risk in Projects, ISBN: 9789699578090.
17. Prof Dr. Javed Iqbal Saani and Muhammad Nadeem Khan (2011, 2018) Understanding Project Management, ISBN: 978969957845, available on amazon (Paperback edition)
18. Prof Dr. Javed Iqbal Saani (2011) Information Systems for Managers, Grass Books, Manchester.
19. Prof Dr. Javed Iqbal Saani (2010) Managing strategic change: a real-world case study, ISBN: 978-3838330952, available on amazon.co.uk. (Paperback edition)

[Please see the images of these books on the following pages in addition to my doctoral thesis]

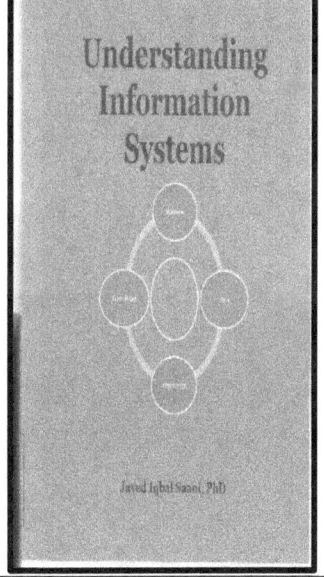

Notes

www.ingramcontent.com/pod-product-compliance
Lightning Source LLC
Chambersburg PA
CBHW071401220526
45469CB00004B/1134